FOOD FOR THOUGHT
AMERICAN ENGLISH IDIOMS

TERESA DELGADILLO-HARRISON

ScottForesman

ISBN: 0-673-19402-7

5678 MAL 97

TABLE OF CONTENTS

Food for Thought presents almost one hundred idioms commonly used by English-speaking North Americans. The idioms presented in this book all include vocabulary related to food and/or eating. They are presented in ten units, clustered around themes that are themselves idiomatic.

In *Food for Thought,* the idioms in each unit are presented and explained in a *Reading*. Because idioms are examples of the informal usage most often found in oral English, the *Readings* include many dialogues. Reading the dialogues aloud will help students get the "feel" of idiomatic English.

Following each *Reading*, the idioms are practiced in *Exercises*. Finally, each unit ends with *Discussion* activities based on the idioms. The *Discussion* gives students an opportunity for oral practice.

Students and instructors will appreciate the variety of ways to use *Food for Thought*. Students can complete units individually, in small groups, or in whole-class sessions. Instructors can spend as much or as little class time on each unit as they feel appropriate.

Some of the idioms are easier to understand and to use than others. They do not have to be explained in great detail or practiced repeatedly. Other idioms require more explanation and practice. Examples of both kinds are included in each unit. Because of this, *Food for Thought*, although designed for intermediate and advanced level students, can be used effectively with advanced beginners as well. It can be used for instructor-led classes or for self-study.

READING

You are learning to speak English, and you want to sound like a native speaker. How can you do this? You can use idioms and slang. These are words or phrases that have different meanings than the ones in the dictionary. For example, you know and use the words *dish* and *out*. When you put these words together, you make an idiom—*to dish out*. This phrase has nothing to do with plates or with the outdoors. **To dish out** can mean "to give in equal parts."

Mom is dishing out the chores.

For another example, nuts are dry, hard-shelled fruit or seeds. The slang word **nuts** can mean several different things. It can mean "excited about something": *I'm nuts about chocolate!* It can also mean "very upset about something": *I almost went nuts when she didn't call.* Another meaning is "crazy, not sane": *He acted nuts when he lost the game.*

Idioms and slang are informal language. You use them with your friends and family. You should not use them in formal letters or in business situations. Here's an example. A slang meaning of **to dish out** is "to criticize." Someone might say, "Todd can dish it out, but he can't take it." This means that Todd often criticizes others, but he becomes angry or hurt when someone criticizes him. You might say this about a fellow student or a friend. You should *not* accuse your teacher or your boss of dishing it out.

As you hear and read more English, you will find more and more idioms. You will read or hear a phrase and understand each individual word. But you might *not* understand the phrase. For example, you might understand each word in the phrase **as cool as a cucumber.** You might not know the meaning "calm; not easily upset."

She's as cool as a cucumber.

If you listen and practice, idioms will become easier for you. You will learn to recognize them and to guess what they mean. Soon you will be using idioms yourself!

Read the following short paragraphs. Think about the meanings of the words in dark type. Then try to figure out the idioms.

1. George is such a **chowderhead**. He *always forgets* to take out the garbage.

2. You *paid too much* for that old car. It's **not worth a hill of beans.**

3. She *went swimming in a frozen lake* on New Year's Day. She's **as nutty as a fruitcake.**

4. His job is *not important.* He's **small potatoes** here.

5. Sam *needs more money,* so he didn't take the job with the circus. It pays **chicken feed.**

Did you see the relationship between each idiom and its meaning?

1. Chowder is soup. You make it with bits and pieces of fish. When you compare a person's head to chowder, you mean that his or her head is full of "bits and pieces" of information. He or she remembers little things, but forgets important things.

2. Beans are an inexpensive food. Even a hill of beans does not cost much money. An old wrecked car is also not worth much money.

3. Swimming in a frozen lake is not a common sport. You probably think that only crazy people do it. Remember that *nuts* can mean "crazy." Fruitcakes are often full of nuts.

4. Potatoes grow under the ground. When you dig up potatoes, you might not see the small ones. They're not very important.

5. Raising chickens can be inexpensive. Chickens can find food almost anywhere. A job that pays chicken feed does not pay much money.

All of these idioms use food words. Food idioms are popular in North American English speech. Why? Probably because food is something that everyone thinks about a lot!

DISCUSSION

1. Does your language use a lot of food idioms? Why do you think this is true?

2. *Nuts* has several meanings. How do you express each one in your language? Do you know an idiom for each meaning?

3. Name something that is not worth a hill of beans. How can you describe this in your language? Do you compare the thing to a kind of food?

4. Do you know someone who is as cool as a cucumber? Who is it? Why did you choose that person? Explain.

DISH IT UP

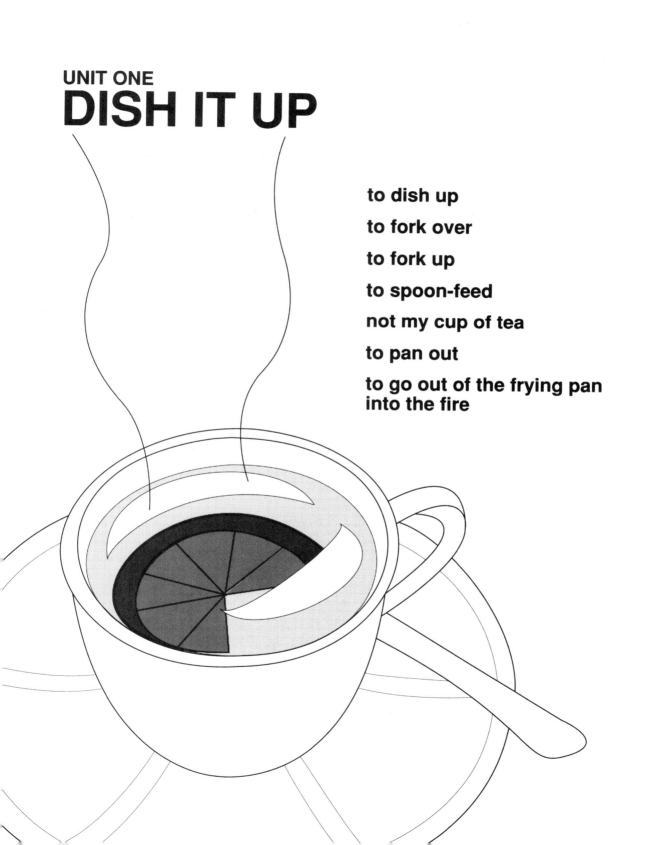

to dish up

to fork over

to fork up

to spoon-feed

not my cup of tea

to pan out

to go out of the frying pan into the fire

READING

An idiom begins as a word or words that everyone understands. Everyone agrees on the meaning. Then someone uses the words with a new meaning. People compare the meanings in their minds. Soon, listeners don't have to make the comparison. They understand the new meaning. An idiom is born.

Many idioms contain the names of kitchen items. Everyone uses dishes, pots and pans, flatware, and glasses. People can easily see these items in their minds. Idioms that use these words are easy to picture, too. For example, the title of this unit is **"Dish It Up."** Can you picture this in your mind? It means "serve" or "put on a dish."

Imagine that you want something badly. You know that another person is carrying that thing. You say, **"Fork it over."**

Fork it over!

If you know that the other person has the item, but he or she *isn't* carrying it, you might say, **"Fork it up."**

You'd better fork it up by tomorrow morning!

This decision table will help you remember when to use these idioms.

If you are:	*and you know:*	*then you say:*
talking to someone face to face	he or she is carrying something that you want	Fork it over.
writing to someone or talking on the telephone	the person has something that you want	Fork it up.
talking to someone face to face	he or she has something that you want, but it's in another place.	Fork it up.

You use these idioms when you are angry or in a hurry. You use them when you are tired of waiting for something. You don't use them in a polite request.

Jan: Where's the TV guide?

Dean: Here it is.

Jan: May I have it, please?

Jan might say *fork it over* when he's angry or when he and Dean are playing.

Jan: Dean, did you take my new record?

Dean: I just borrowed it to listen to a song.

Jan: Fork it over! I told you not to play my records. You always scratch them!

Note that you can say, "Fork it (up/over)" or "Fork (up/over) the (money)."

Someone usually feeds a baby or a sick person with a spoon. The idiom **to spoon-feed** means "to give or tell a little at a time" or "to indulge." This idiom can be unkind. It can mean that a person is foolish or helpless.

Michele: Did you finish writing the report?

Chris: No. I'm having trouble with the computer again.

Michele: You always have the same excuse! I'm tired of spoon-feeding you the same directions every week!

Here is another example. This time the idiom is not unkind.

Burt: Are you still having trouble with those math problems?

Loni: Yes. You'll have to spoon-feed me until I get them right.

In the first example, Michele is making fun of Chris. In the second example, Loni is making fun of herself. Which example has a stronger effect on the person who needs help?

People express their likes and dislikes in many ways. Idioms are an interesting way to do this. When people don't like something, they might say, "It's **not my cup of tea**." They are not talking about something to drink. They are expressing a mild dislike.

Pat: Do you want to go to the Opera Hall on Saturday? They're playing a new American opera.

Vanna: I'd rather go to a rock concert. Opera is not my cup of tea.

That was a friendly conversation. The dislike was clear, but it didn't bother anybody. In the following example, two people are upset. Angry people do not use the idiom *not my cup of tea*.

Father: You're going to boarding school next year! Maybe your grades and your behavior will improve.

Daughter: No, I'm not! I hate boarding school! I'll run away!

When a plan fails, a person might say, "It didn't pan out." **To pan out** means "to get good results." This is an old idiom. Years ago, people used pans to look for gold in rivers. If things panned out, you struck it rich!

Joanne: The band is going to have a cookie sale. We want to raise money for our trip. Our plans to have a talent show didn't pan out.

Fred: I hope the sale pans out. We need a lot of money for the trip.

Think about your favorite adventure movie or TV show. The hero or heroine escapes from danger. Then, a few minutes later, he or she meets another danger. That person has gone **out of the frying pan into the fire**.

Heroine: Thank goodness our horses jumped over that canyon. The bandits almost caught us.

Hero: Don't look now, but there are wolves all around us! We went out of the frying pan into the fire.

What happens when food falls out the pan and into the fire? It burns!

Did you notice that the meanings of these kitchen-item idioms have nothing to do with cooking or food? That's the way of idioms. An idiom uses a familiar word in a new way.

EXERCISES

A. Select the best idiom to complete each sentence. You may use an idiom more than once.

a. fork it over

b. fork it up

c. spoon-feed

d. not my cup of tea

e. pan out

f. out of the frying pan into the fire

g. dish up

1. Trudy will never learn. She lent Saks ten dollars last month, and he didn't repay the money. Now she's going to lend him ten more. She always goes ___**f**___.

2. Johnny can't remember how to play Parcheesi. I have to _____ him the rules every time we play.

3. I'm tired of waiting for the money that you owe me. I want it now! You'd better _____ by tonight!

4. We had a terrible storm on Saturday. We had to cancel our picnic. Our plans just didn't _____.

5. You can't get away now! I see the stolen necklace in your pocket. You'd better _____.

6. I like summer sports because I like warm weather. Winter sports are _____.

7. After I broke my leg skiing, I tried a less dangerous sport—ice skating. I broke my ankle during my first lesson. I went _____.

8. Okay, class, whoever has my answer key had better _____, or I'll fail everybody!

9. I tried to make photographic film for my chemistry project, but it didn't _____. The chemicals were too old.

10. We're almost ready to eat. Please _____ the vegetables.

B. Write *yes* or *no* after each sentence.

He dished up the soup.
Did he put it in bowls?   ___**Yes.**___

1. Tom's idea didn't pan out.
   Was Tom successful?   _____

2. Golf is not Cindy's cup of tea.
   Does Cindy like to play golf?   _____

3. Jerry always goes out of the frying pan
   into the fire.
   Does Jerry have bad luck? _____

4. Laura always spoon-feeds the answers to Bill.
   Does Bill need a lot of help? _____

5. The police told the robber to fork over the jewels.
   Is the robber holding the jewels? _____

6. Betty told John to fork up the money.
   Is John holding the money? _____

DISCUSSION

1. Think of a movie or a TV show in which the hero
   or heroine went out of the frying pan into the
   fire. Describe it to the class.

2. Make a list of five things you like. Label the list
   My Cup of Tea. Make a list of five things you
   don't like. Label the list *Not My Cup of Tea.*
   Share the lists with your classmates. Do you like
   and dislike the same things?

3. Did you ever have to spoon-feed someone? Tell the
   class about it.

4. Look in an encyclopedia for the biography of a
   great inventor or scientist. (You might choose
   Marie Curie, Thomas Edison, or George
   Washington Carver.) Describe one of his or
   her early experiments that didn't pan out.

5. Write six sentences that could end with *fork it up*
   or *fork it over.* Read each sentence and ask your
   classmates to select the correct idiom.

SUGAR AND SPICE

the salt of the earth

to take it with a grain of salt

sugar/honey

(one's) bread and butter

to know which side (one's) bread is buttered on

a bread-and-butter letter

a butterfingers

to add some spice to your life

READING

An old nursery rhyme says, "Sugar and spice and everything nice—that's what little girls are made of." We often use food idioms to describe people.

Do you trust a lot of people? Why do you trust certain people? Do they always tell the truth? Do they keep secrets? Do they keep promises? Trustworthy people do those things. Do you *not* trust anyone? Why? You can use idioms to describe both kinds of people.

When you trust someone, you depend on that person. Salt is necessary to life. We depend on it. When you say that a person is **the salt of the earth**, you mean that you can depend on the person.

Patti: LaVerne is a wonderful person! She took care of my kids for a week when I was sick.

Maxine: She did the same thing for me. She's the salt of the earth.

Who do you not trust? Salt can describe that person, too. **To take it with a grain of salt** means "to not believe everything that someone says."

Ron: Did you hear that Pete had six dates this weekend?

Don: Did Pete say that? You should take it with a grain of salt. He always makes up big stories.

Sugar and honey taste sweet. When you call someone **sugar** or **honey**, you are saying that the person is "sweet" (likeable and agreeable). We say these words when we love someone.

Sara: Honey, I'm going to go fly our airplane for a while.

Andy: Okay, sugar. I'll make lunch when you get back.

These words should never be used in a formal situation. They should never be said to strangers. Here are two ways you should *not* use them.

Boss: Would you get me some coffee, honey.

Secretary: The coffee is right behind you, ma'am. And my name is Winston, not honey!

Man: Hi, sugar. Where have you been all my
life?

Molly: Holly, did you hear someone talking to us?

Holly: No, I didn't. I just heard a lot of wind.

In the first example, *honey* is too personal. It is not
professional. It makes the secretary feel like a servant
and not like a co-worker. In the second example, the
man is rude. He doesn't know the women. If he wants
to talk to them, he should introduce himself politely.

Several food idioms use the words *bread* and *butter*.
Bread and butter are important foods. Bread is as
common as salt. People call bread "the staff of life."
This means that bread is necessary to life. Butter adds
fat to the diet. Bread tastes good with butter on it.

Put the importance of bread and butter together.
You will understand these idioms easily.

Diana: What's Mary doing these days? I never
see her.

Shirley: She works for her bread and butter during the day, and she goes to school at night.

Diana: I hope things pan out for her. She really works hard!

Did you understand that Mary is working for money? **Her bread and butter** means "the money that she needs to live."

To know which side your bread is buttered on means "to know that something is good for you." For example, you might treat someone in a special way because you want something from that person.

Bianca: Why is Jerry always with the boss? He eats lunch with him every day. And he agrees with everything that the boss says.

Mick: Don't you know? He wants a promotion. He knows which side his bread is buttered on!

After you eat a meal at someone's house or stay at someone's house for a while, you write a thank-you note. Some people call this **a bread-and-butter letter.**

Ron: Did the mail come, honey?

Nancy: Yes. And look at this!

Ron: What is it?

Nancy: It's a bread-and-butter letter from Maureen. She's thanking us for dinner—two years ago!

Don't be like Maureen. Send your bread-and-butter letter in a few days—not two years later!

When you have butter on your hands, your hands are slippery. If you try to pick something up, you'll drop it. A person who is **a butterfingers** always drops things.

Shelly: Ted, did you drop the dishes again?

Ted: I'm sorry. I'll try to be more careful.

Shelly: You said that yesterday. You're such a butterfingers! I have to spend all my money on new dishes!

You don't have to have butter on your hands to be a butterfingers!

Now add some spice to your life with these exercises. (Spice makes food taste better. **To add some spice to your life** means "to make your life more interesting.")

I told you that skiing would add some spice to your life!

A. What do you say? Choose the correct sentence.

Laura shouldn't believe that story.

(a.) She should take it with a grain of salt.

b. She should add some spice to her life.

1. Carl is very trustworthy.

    a. He's a butterfingers.

    b. He's the salt of the earth.

2. Chris needs a job.

    a. She wants to write a bread-and-butter letter.

    b. She wants to earn her bread and butter.

3. Peter always flatters his boss.

    a. Peter knows which side his bread is buttered on.

    b. Peter takes it with a grain of salt.

4. Ellen stays home and watches TV every night.

    a. She should write a bread-and-butter letter.

    b. She should add some spice to her life.

5. You love someone. That person does something for you.

    a. Thanks, honey.

    b. Thanks, butterfingers.

B. Complete the sentence with one of the idioms. You may use an idiom more than once.

sugar/honey

a butterfingers

the salt of the earth

bread and butter

a bread-and-butter letter

take it with a grain of salt

know which side your bread is buttered on

add some spice to your life.

He: Did you do all the gardening?

She: Yes, I know you're tired today.

He: Thanks, **sugar** _____.

1. I lost my paycheck. Jack lent me some money.

   Jack is _____.

2. Toni went out of the frying pan into the fire. First she was late for the boss's dinner. Then she forgot to thank him. Toni should write _____

   _____.

3. Mrs. Jones is a popular teacher. She spoon-feeds her algebra class. Her students depend on her.

   Mrs. Jones is _____.

4. Carl can't hold on to anything. He's _____

   _____.

5. You insulted your boss? Don't you _____

   _____?

6. Tim is looking for a job. He wants to earn his

   _____.

7. Did "late Nate" tell you that he'll be on time?

   You should _____.

8. Leave me alone! I don't know you, and I am *not*

   your _____!

9. Let's go skydiving this weekend. You work too

   hard. You should _____

   _____.

10. Hi, _____. I'm home. What's

    for dinner?

DISCUSSION

1. Go the the library and find a book of quotations. Select two or three that contain the word *salt, bread,* or *butter.* Share them with the class. What do the quotations mean?

2. Think about spices that were important in history. (Some of them are salt, pepper, nutmeg, and saffron.) Why do you think they were important? Tell the class.

3. Select one idiom from this unit. Write a short dialogue that uses the idiom. Ask a classmate to say the dialogue with you. Does the class understand the dialogue?

4. As a class, rewrite one or more of the dialogues from this unit. Do not use idioms. Which dialogues do you like better—the ones with the idioms or the ones without the idioms?

5. Someone you don't know very well, or someone you don't like, calls you "honey." How can you tell the person to stop? Discuss with the class.

6. Start a class bulletin board, wall chart, or other display for idioms. When you hear or read a new one, put it on the board. Discuss each new idiom in class. What do you think it means?

UNIT THREE
"FOWL PLAY"

a goose egg

to cook (one's) goose

to talk turkey

to quit cold turkey

chicken / to chicken out

to eat like a bird

duck soup / a piece of cake

to count (one's) chickens before they hatch

READING

A fowl is a bird. Birds have feathers and lay eggs. Birds' eggs are many different sizes. A hummingbird egg is tiny. An ostrich egg is huge. A goose egg is large and round. It looks like a zero (0). *Zero* means "nothing." When someone gets **a goose egg**, he or she fails or gets nothing.

Geoffrey: What did you get on the calculus test?

Bob: It was a total failure. I got a goose egg! Zero!

Geoffrey: Don't worry. We have three more tests. You'll do better next time.

Bob: Oh, no! Three more chances for goose eggs!

Another meaning of **goose egg** is "swelling from an injury."

Muffy: Where did you get that goose egg on your head?

Buffy: I was in the library. I reached for a dictionary, and four books fell on my head!

Imagine that you got into trouble, and it was your fault. No one did anything to you. You did it to yourself. You **cooked your own goose.**

Sandy: I lost a lot of money today. I made a mistake when I traded some stocks.

Teresa: What happened? Did someone give you bad advice?

Sandy: No, I was careless. I cooked my own goose.

You can also cook someone else's goose.

Mandy: Steve never does his homework. He always wants to copy mine.

Andy: What are you going to do about it?

Mandy: I'm going to cook his goose. I'm going to give him all the wrong answers!

A lot of times, you and your friends probably talk about things that are not very important. You make "small talk." Other times, you talk seriously. When you want to talk seriously to someone, you can say, "Let's **talk turkey**."

Temple: Where do you want to go on vacation?

Shirley: Australia!

Temple: Let's talk turkey. We have only five hundred dollars. We can go as far as Idaho, if we're lucky!

Shirley: I know. I was just dreaming.

A cold turkey might shiver and feel uncomfortable. **To quit cold turkey** means "to break a habit or stop an addiction without medical help." People who are addicted to drugs sometimes quit cold turkey. They often become sick and shiver for a while.

Manny: I heard that you quit smoking.

Lew: Yes. It was very hard.

Manny: Did you go to a doctor for help?

Lew: No, I did it by myself. I quit cold turkey!

Many people believe that chickens are always afraid. Some idioms compare people to frightened chickens. A **chicken** is a person who is afraid to do something new or exciting. **To chicken out** means "to stop because you are frightened."

Doug: Come on. Let's jump off this cliff into the river.

Jim: Not me! This cliff is too high, and that river is too shallow!

Doug: Come on, chicken. You won't get hurt. You never want to try anything!

Joe: We're going to ski in the dark tonight. We'll meet you at eight o'clock.

Marilyn: I'm not going.

Joe: Oh, Marilyn, don't chicken out.

Marilyn: I'm not a good skier. You go, and I'll see you later.

These idioms are insulting. Sometimes it's all right to be afraid. It's not polite to call frightened people chickens or to say that they chickened out.

Some people think that birds don't each much, but scientists know that birds eat a lot. In one day, a bird eats as much as it weighs! However, the idiom **to eat like a bird** means "to eat very little."

Charles: You should eat more, honey.

Diana: But I'm not hungry.

Charles: I know, but you're too thin. You eat like
a bird.

Duck soup is probably easy to make. The idiom
duck soup means "easy to do."

Claus: How's the new job? It sounds like hard work.

Donner: Hard work? It's duck soup! I pull a sled full
of toys, but I only work one night a year!

The idiom **a piece of cake** means the same as
duck soup.

Gary: Did you finish the *New York Times* Crossword
Puzzle already?

Jane: It was a piece of cake! I did it in fifteen minutes.

Gary: That's great! I tried for two hours!

Do you understand these idioms? Then try the
exercise. But **don't count your chickens before
they hatch**. (That means, "don't be over-confident;
don't believe something until it happens.")

By the way, did you understand the title of this unit? *Foul* means "dirty" or "evil." A detective in a story might say, "The butler is dead, and it looks like foul play." The detective means that something bad or violent happened. *Fowl* and *foul* sound alike. *Fowl play* is not an idiom. It's a pun or a play on words.

EXERCISES

A. Write *yes* or *no*.

You have a goose egg on your forehead.
Does your head hurt? __**Yes.**__

1. You got a goose egg on the history test.
    Did you pass? _____

2. You wanted to talk turkey.
    Were you serious? _____

3. You cooked your own goose.
    Was it your fault? _____

4. You quit cold turkey.
    Did you go to the doctor? _____

5. You chickened out.
    Were you afraid? _____

6. You ate like a bird.
    Did you eat a lot? _____

7. It was a piece of cake.
    Was it easy? _____

8. You counted your chickens before they hatched.
    Were you over-confident? _____

9. You did something brave.
    Were you chicken? _____

10. The test was duck soup.
    Did you pass? _____

B. What does each person say? Complete each sentence with one of the idioms. You may use an idiom more than once.

a goose egg

chicken

duck soup/a piece of cake

to cook your own goose

to talk turkey

to quit cold turkey

to eat like a bird

to count your chickens before they hatch

to chicken out

Bill got an *A* on the test. What did he say?
"It was **a piece of cake**_____."

1. Pat is talking about a movie. Dick wants to talk

   about business. What does Dick say?

   "I want _____."

2. Bob wants to stop smoking. He doesn't want to

   see a doctor. What does he say?

   "I'm going _____."

3. Marge bought a lottery ticket. When she wins,

   she's going to buy a diamond bracelet. What do

   her friends tell her?

   "You're foolish _____

   _____."

4. The road is very icy. Barb doesn't want to drive.

    Her friends think she's afraid. What do they say?

    "Barb, you're a _____."

5. Fred and Imelda are decorating the gym for a

    dance. Fred hates to decorate. He asks Imelda to

    do it all. What does she answer?

    "Sure, Fred, it's _____."

6. Phil thinks that Elizabeth is the salt of the earth.

    She is always serious and businesslike. What does

    Phil say about her?

    "You can trust Elizabeth _____

    _____."

7. Stan is a butterfingers. He just dropped a very

    expensive vase. What does Oliver say to him?

    "Stan, that's the way _____

    _____."

8. Fernando's baseball team does not play well.

    Today, they didn't score at all. What does

    Fernando tell Reggie?

    "Reggie, we got _____."

9. Mario will not drive too fast. The man in the next car wants to race. Mario refuses. What do his friends say?

   "Mario, you were smart _____

   _____."

10. Mary Beth is always on a diet. Christine is thin, but she never diets. What does Mary Beth say to her friend?

    "I try _____,

    but I still gain weight!"

DISCUSSION

1. Write a list of animals. Use the list to make up phrases about eating; for example, he eats like a snake (slowly); she eats like a horse (a lot). Ask your classmates to guess the meanings of your phrases.

2. You refuse to do something dangerous, and someone says that you are a chicken. What do you say?

3. Some other expressions for failing are *down the drain, down the tubes, a washout*, and *a flop*. Discuss these phrases with the class. Do you understand them?

4. Write a dialogue using one or more of the idioms in this unit. Share it with the class. Did you use the idioms correctly?

5. Do you know any "bird idioms" in a language other than English? Share them and their meanings with the class.

6. Use the phrase *as rare as a* . . . to make up "idioms." Use the names of birds and animals to complete the phrase. For example: *As rare as a bald eagle.* (Bald eagles are almost extinct.) *As rare as a dodo bird.* (Dodos are extinct.) Explain your "idioms" to the class.

(one's) bread and butter	to add some spice to your life
a bread-and-butter letter	to chicken out
a butterfingers	to cook (one's) own goose
a chicken	to count (one's) chickens before they hatch
chicken feed	to dish up/out
a chowderhead	to eat like a bird
duck soup	to fork over/up
a goose egg	to go out of the frying pan into the fire
a piece of cake	to know which side (one's) bread is buttered on
the salt of the earth	
small potatoes	to pan out
sugar/honey	to quit cold turkey
as cool as a cucumber	to spoon-feed
as nutty as a fruit cake	to take it with a grain of salt
not my cup of tea	to talk turkey
not worth a hill of beans	
nuts	

A. Circle the correct answer.

EXERCISES

Who often forgets things?

(a.) a chowderhead

b. a chicken

1. Who is afraid to try something new or dangerous?

   a. a chicken

   b. a butterfingers

2. What is easy to do?

   a. a piece of cake

   b. a hill of beans

3. Which describes a thank-you note?

   a. spoon-feed

   b. bread-and-butter

4. What do you call someone you love?

   a. salt

   b. sugar

5. What does a teacher do with homework?

   a. pan out

   b. dish out

6. Who always drops things?

   a. a butterfingers

   b. a chowderhead

7. Which describes something that you don't like?

   a. not worth a hill of beans

   b. not my cup of tea

8. Whom can you depend on?

   a. the salt of the earth

   b. your bread and butter

9. Which describes something that turns out well?

   a. to go out of the frying pan into the fire.

   b. to pan out

10. How do you help someone?

    a. spoon-feed

    b. chicken out

B. Match the idiom with its meaning.

__c__	1.	a small amount of money
_____	2.	to get into trouble through your own fault
_____	3.	not sane
_____	4.	easy to do
_____	5.	not easily upset
_____	6.	to give
_____	7.	not to do something because of fear
_____	8.	nothing
_____	9.	to believe something before it happens
_____	10.	to eat very little

a. as cool as a cucumber

b. as nutty as a fruitcake

c. chicken feed

d. duck soup

e. a goose egg

f. to count your chickens before they hatch

g. to cook your own goose

h. to fork over

i. to chicken out

j. to eat like a bird

C. Rewrite each sentence. Use an idiom in place of the underlined words.

The algebra test was <u>easy</u>. I got 100%.

The algebra test was duck soup. _____

1. George is <u>trustworthy and dependable</u>.

   _____

   _____

2. "<u>I don't like</u> jogging," said Mickey.

   _____

   _____

3. Mary Jane doesn't smoke. She <u>stopped without</u>
   <u>any help</u>.

   _____

4. He thinks he's important, but he's really
   <u>unimportant</u>.

   _____

   _____

5. We planned a picnic, but it didn't <u>happen</u>.

   _____

   _____

6. You should <u>do something interesting</u>. Try
   skydiving.

   _____

7. Maria said she won a million dollars? <u>Don't</u>
   <u>believe everything she says</u>.

   _____

8. Stop joking! I want <u>to talk seriously</u>!

   _____

9. Nora always does nice things for the boss. She
   <u>knows who is important here</u>!

   _____

   _____

10. Chris went through a stop sign. Then he ran into
    a police car. He always <u>goes from one bad thing</u>
    <u>to another</u>.

    _____

    _____

UNIT FOUR
AN APPLE
A DAY

apple polisher / apple
polishing

to compare apples
and oranges

the apple of (one's) eye

one bad apple spoils
the barrel

in apple-pie order

as American as apple pie

to get to the core of (something)

READING

Apples are a common and popular fruit in the United States. People believe that apples are good for you. They say, "An apple a day keeps the doctor away." (In this saying, *a* means "every.") Many English idioms mention apples. This information will help you understand the idioms in this unit.

1. Apple skins shine when you rub them.

2. You can keep apples in a barrel in a cool place. They stay fresh for a long time.

3. In many stores, you can choose apples one at a time. People choose the apples that look the best.

4. Apple pie is a common American dessert. People think that apple pies look pretty and taste delicious.

Did you ever take a gift to your teacher? Children in the United States often bring apples for their teachers. They polish the apples, so the skins shine. Some people might think that these apples are bribes. They think that the students want better grades. An **apple polisher** is a person who does nice things because he or she wants special treatment.

Jerry: May I type those letters for you, sir?

Dean: Of course. And please get me some coffee.

Martin: Why is Jerry doing all your work?

Dean: He's a real apple polisher. He thinks I'll give him a raise.

Poor Jerry doesn't know that Dean is taking advantage of him. **Apple polishing** doesn't always work.

Apples and oranges are very different. **To compare apples and oranges** means "to compare two things that are very different." In fact, they are so different that you should *not* compare them.

B. Bunny: I got here in ten minutes. I won the race!

T. Turtle: Don't be silly! You're comparing apples and oranges! You drove a car, and I rode a bike!

Imagine that you are in a store. You want a nice, crisp apple. You look at all the apples, and you choose the one that looks the best. To be **the apple of someone's eye** means to be that person's favorite—the one he or she likes best.

Jim: Hi, honey. I'm home. Where's Samantha?

Jane: She's playing outside. The apple of your eye is playing football with the boys.

Jim: That's my girl! She's the best football player in the neighborhood!

A child is often the apple of his or her parents' eye. A good student might be the apple of a teacher's eye.

One rotten or spoiled piece of fruit can spoil all the fruit around it. Bacteria spoil food. Bacteria spread in the air from one piece of fruit to the others. But when we say **one bad apple spoils the barrel,** we are usually talking about people, not fruit. One person can encourage other people to do something wrong.

Mr. Hyde: Where is everybody? Lunch hour is over!

Ms. Jeckel: Everybody went birdwatching with Mr. Frank. They take longer and longer lunches every day.

Mr. Hyde: I'm going to fire Mr. Frank! Before he came here, people took only one hour for lunch. Now they take two hours. One bad apple spoils the barrel!

Did you understand that birdwatching is not wrong? Mr. Hyde is angry because his employees take too long for lunch. He believes that it's Mr. Frank's fault. (Mr. Frank cooked his own goose!)

Apple pie is a very popular dessert in the United States. To make an apple pie, you mix apples and sugar and bake them in a shallow pastry crust. People usually decorate the top of an apple pie.

When something is neat and clean, you can say it's **in apple-pie order.**

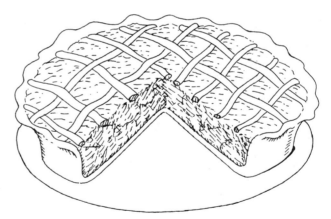

Mother: Did you clean up the living room?

Son: Yes, I did. It's in apple-pie order. May I go to the movies now?

Mother: You'd better. I want that room to stay neat for a while!

This idiom can also mean "everything is ready" or "the plans are complete."

Scott: Is everything ready for the golf tournament?

Howard: Yes. Everything is in apple-pie order. I just
          hope it doesn't rain, or the tournament won't
          pan out.

Apple pie can be a symbol of America. We can say
that something is **as American as apple pie.** This
means that everyone knows that it is from the United
States. Everyone recognizes that it is distinctly
American.

Gloria: I love your new designs. They're practical and
          attractive.

Ralph: Thank you. I like the "cowboy look."

Gloria: So do I. It's as American as apple pie.

Henri: I had a wonderful French lunch. I had a roll
          with ground beef, cheese, and lettuce.

Henry: Henri, you ate a hamburger! That's not
          French! It's as American as apple pie.

Is that enough about apples and apple pie? The
exercises will get to the core of the lesson. (The center
of an apple is the core. **To get to the core of**
something means "to get to the most important part.")

EXERCISES   **A. Circle the sentence that answers the question.**

How might a proud father describe his new baby daughter?

a. She's as American as apple pie.

b. She's the apple of my eye.

1. How might a teacher describe a boy who causes trouble?

   a. He's as American as apple pie.

   b. One bad apple spoils the barrel.

2. Tom is talking about caviar. Mary is talking about canned tuna. What are they doing?

   a. They're comparing apples and oranges.

   b. They're apple polishing.

3. How might you describe a dresser drawer in which everything is neat and clean?

   a. It's as American as apple pie.

   b. It's in apple-pie order.

4. Jerry thinks that his parents love his sister more than they love him. How might he describe his sister?

   a. One bad apple spoils the barrel.

   b. She's the apple of their eye.

5. How might you describe a Fourth-of-July picnic?

   a. It's the apple of my eye.

   b. It's as American as apple pie.

6. Everyone in Mr. Phelps' department is dissatisfied. Mr. Phelps is talking to each person individually. He wants to find out what's wrong. What is he trying to do?

   a. He's trying to get to the core of the problem.

   b. He's trying to compare apples and oranges.

7. Louis laughs at all the boss's jokes. He pays the boss compliments every day. How might you describe Louis?

    a. He's in apple-pie order.

    b. He's an apple polisher.

8. How might a TV announcer describe a World Series baseball game?

    a. It's apple polishing.

    b. It's as American as apple pie.

9. June said that her lunch at the hot-dog stand cost two dollars. Ralph said that his lunch at the Ritz cost sixty dollars. What are they doing?

    a. They're getting to the core of the argument.

    b. They're comparing apples and oranges.

10. Years ago, Betty Lee went to prison for robbery. Now she wants a job at a bank. What might the bank president say?

    a. She's the apple of my eye.

    b. One bad apple spoils the barrel.

B. Complete the sentence with one of the idioms.

the apple of my eye   as American as apple pie
apple polisher   comparing apples and oranges
in apple-pie order   get to the core of

I like the cowboy look.
It's **as American as apple pie**   .

1. Teresa is my favorite student.

    She's _____.

2. Timmy always brings flowers for his teacher.

    He's an _____.

3. Carmen is talking about her moped. Jill is

   talking about her jet.

   They're _____.

4. Mrs. Jones cleaned the whole house today.

   It's _____.

5. Jimmy and Billy were fighting. Mr. Johnson

   wants to know why.

   He wants to _____ the

   argument.

DISCUSSION

1. Think of three things in your life that are in apple-pie order. Describe them to the class.

2. Think of other ways to complete this idiom: *one bad _____ spoils the _____*. Explain your choices to the class.

3. Use the idioms in this unit to play Charades. Divide the class into two teams. The person who guesses the other team's charade first does the next charade.

4. Think of something that is typical of your country. Complete the idiom *as _____ as _____*. Share it with the class. (Example: as Japanese as sushi.)

5. Do you know an apple polisher? Tell the class about that person, but don't say the person's name. Say, "I know a person who. . . ."

6. Who might be the apple of someone's eye? Think of as many examples as possible. Compare your answers with your classmates'.

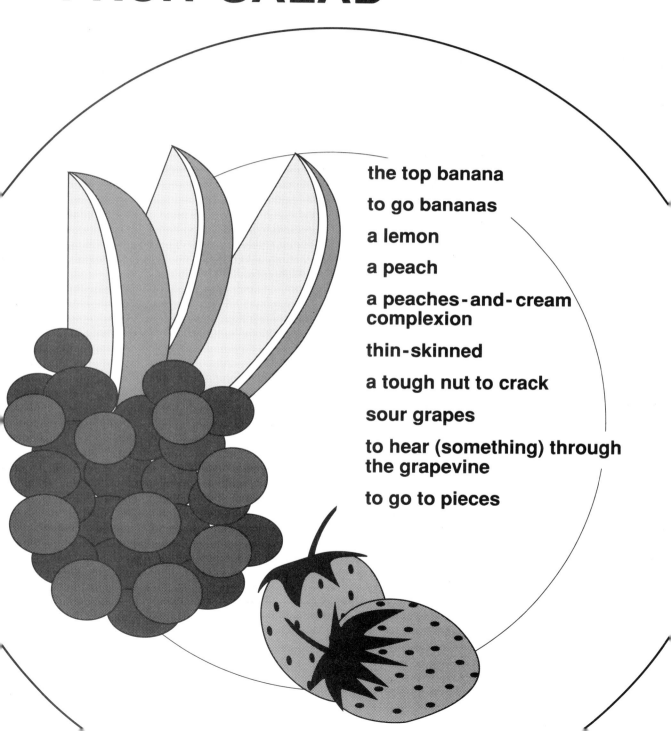

UNIT FIVE

FRUIT SALAD

the top banana

to go bananas

a lemon

a peach

a peaches-and-cream complexion

thin-skinned

a tough nut to crack

sour grapes

to hear (something) through the grapevine

to go to pieces

READING

Are you ready for more fruit idioms? Pretend that your class is putting on a comedy show. You are the star comedian. What do people call you? They might call you **the top banana.** This idiom can also describe the most important person in a group.

Franny: Is that Mr. Seymour, the famous business man?

Zooey: Yes, it is. He's the top banana in our company, and the richest man in town.

When you **go bananas,** you get very upset about something. You might act nuts.

Frank: Why do you always talk to other men at parties?

Ava: Don't go bananas, Frank. That was my Uncle Sam.

Frank: I'm sorry. I go nuts when I see you with someone else.

You might also go bananas when you are very excited and happy about something.

Warp: What's going on? You two are going totally bananas.

Ivy: You won't believe it!

Fleur: We have tickets to the Ungrateful Mummies concert!

Warp: Hey, that's a good reason to go bananas!

Lemons taste very sour. People don't usually eat lemons as fruit. They use lemons to make lemonade or to flavor other foods. The idiom **a lemon** means "something that gives you a bad feeling or taste."

Roslyn: Why don't you drive your car?

Amy: It won't start. It's a lemon.

Roslyn: Can't you take it back?

Amy: The guarantee was a lemon, too. It was for only ten days!

Peaches taste sweet. They have soft, pink and gold skins. A person who is **a peach** is a honey, the salt of the earth.

Robert: Honey, will you take these books to the library for me? I don't have time.

Natalie: Sure.

Robert: You're a peach. I'll do a favor for you
         sometime.

Natalie: Okay. Be a peach and make dinner tonight.

A dish of sliced peaches in cream is a delicious
dessert. The colors of the peaches and the cream look
beautiful. A person with **a peaches-and-cream
complexion** has beautiful skin. It is soft and smooth,
and it has a pretty, fresh color.

Matt: Did you see the new girl in our history class?

Mike: Yes. She's gorgeous!

Matt: Her skin is beautiful. My mom calls that a
       peaches-and-cream complexion.

Mike: If that means "pretty," your mom is right!

Peaches and many other fruits have thin skins.
They bruise or spot easily. Some people are **thin-
skinned.** They get upset easily. It's easy to hurt their
feelings. You can insult them without meaning to.

Debbie: Don't be upset, sugar. Richard was just
         kidding. He doesn't really think that you're a
         chowderhead.

Eddie: I know. I guess I'm too thin-skinned.

Other kinds of fruit have thick skins. Nuts are
thick-skinned fruits. Did you ever try to crack a nut
with your teeth? It's difficult! A difficult person or
thing can be **a tough nut to crack.**

Mr. Wright: Did you sell those computers to the
             Acme Company?

Ms. True: No. Mr. Acme is a tough nut to crack.
           He wants to see another demonstration
           next week.

Mr. Wright: Well, keep trying. I think you're close to
             a sale.

Grapes grow on vines. The vines grow fast and spread over long distances. Gossip can spread as quickly and as far as a grapevine. **To hear (something) through the grapevine** means "to hear something from someone who heard it from someone else who heard it from someone else...."

Dr. Ruth: Did you hear that Dr. Jones is getting married?

Dr. Joyce: No! Did you read it in the hospital newspaper?

Dr. Ruth: The paper doesn't come out until Friday. I heard it through the grapevine. You know how gossip spreads around here.

Did you ever hear something through the grapevine? People usually spread rumors that way.

A famous story tells about a fox who sees some grapes. The fox is hungry, but the grapes are growing very high. When the fox can't reach them, it says, "Oh, well. They're probably sour anyway." The idiom **sour grapes** means "pretending you dislike something because you can't have it."

Kathy: Why isn't Jan going to the junior class dance?

Cindy: She's angry because they didn't elect her president of the class.

Kathy: That's sour grapes. She'll miss all the fun!

A fruit salad contains pieces of different kinds of fruit. Don't you **go to pieces** (get upset about something bad) when you do the exercises.

A. Circle the correct idiom to complete each sentence.

EXERCISES

Mary always cries when I correct her. She's

a. thin-skinned.

b. a lemon.

1. Marti's friend told her that Jane was promoted. Marti

   a. heard it through the grapevine.

   b. was thin-skinned.

2. Mrs. Masters is the president of the company. She's

   a. a lemon.

   b. the top banana.

3. When Hank won the prize, he

   a. said it was sour grapes.

   b. went bananas.

4. Mrs. Young is eighty years old, but her skin is still beautiful. She

   a. went to pieces.

   b. has a peaches-and-cream complexion.

5. Mr. Hulk never gets upset. He's not

   a. a peach.

   b. thin-skinned.

6. I bought a new vacuum cleaner, but it doesn't work. It's

   a. sour grapes.

   b. a lemon.

7. Mrs. Smith loves Mr. Smith. She thinks he's

   a. a lemon.

   b. a peach.

8. The spy didn't give any information to the police. He was

   a. thin-skinned.

   b. a tough nut to crack.

9. Trudy's boyfriend broke up with her. Now she says terrible things about him. Everyone knows

   a. he's the top banana.

   b. it's sour grapes.

10. Sam loves Mary. When she was away on her vacation, he was so lonesome that he almost

   a. was the top banana.

   b. went to pieces.

B. Complete the sentence with one of the idioms.

| a peach | the top banana | thin-skinned |
| a lemon | a tough nut to crack | sour grapes |

Ted didn't get the job he wanted. Now he says he never wanted it.
It's __sour grapes_____.

1. He's the star of the show.

   He's _____.

2. This car is not worth a hill of beans!

   It's _____.

3. The boss never laughs at my jokes.

   He's _____.

4. She's the salt of the earth.

   She's _____.

5. Bob gets insulted very easily.

   He's _____.

DISCUSSION

1. Think of other ways to describe someone's complexion. Share them with the class.

2. Do you know a "fruit idiom" in a language other than English? Tell the class. (Describe the feel and taste of the fruit if the class is not familiar with it.)

3. Make a list of thin-skinned fruits. How do you handle those fruits? How do you handle thin-skinned people? Make a comparison.

4. Make a list of people you know who are tough nuts to crack. Tell the class about one of the people. (Don't tell the person's name.)

5. Go to an encyclopedia and look up one kind of fruit. Write a paragraph about that fruit and read it to the class. If you know an idiom that mentions that fruit, try to explain it.

SOUP'S ON

to beef up

to ham it up

a ham

to make a pig of (oneself)

to have other fish to fry

a hot dog

a hot potato

to spill the beans

an egghead

READING

Soup's on means "the food is ready, come and eat." This unit dishes up idioms that sound like dinner, but they're not about food.

To beef up means "to add to" or "to make stronger." You beef something up to make it better.

Coach: Our tennis team is terrible this year. We have to beef it up.

Assistant: Watch those two freshmen. They play very well.

Coach: Great! Let's ask them to try out for the team.

Dr. Vincent: This mixture isn't correct. The chemicals aren't working right.

Dr. Price: Let's beef up the formula with some more sulfuric acid.

Note that you can say "beef up (the team)" or "beef it up."

When you **ham it up,** you exaggerate your movements. People usually ham it up to be funny.

Dave: Look at Phil. Did you ever see anybody hit a golf ball like that?

Arlo: He always hams it up when people are watching.

Actors who are very dramatic and exaggerate their voices and movements are **hams.**

Principal: I enjoyed the school play. Arthur Moore is really a ham.

Teacher: He's a ham in class, too. He always makes everyone laugh.

People think that pigs are dirty and that pigs eat a lot. It's not nice to compare a person to a pig.

Crocker: May I have another piece of pie?

Betty: You've had four pieces already! You're **making a pig of yourself!**

Crocker: I can't help it. You're a wonderful cook!

When you have **other fish to fry,** you have other things to do.

Jaime: Do you want to study with me tonight?

Hawk: No. I have tickets to the rock concert.

Jaime: You always have other fish to fry.

Hawk: Well, you only live once!

A hot dog is as American as apple pie. The expression **hot dog** can show excitement. When you go bananas because something makes you happy, you might say, "Hot dog!"

Announcer: Pax is running toward the end zone. The
pass is going toward him. He's falling!
No! Hot dog! He caught the ball! It's a
touchdown! The Mustangs win!

Hot dog can also describe someone who shows off.
Other people don't always like a hot dog.

Pete: Porfirio doesn't give anyone else a chance to
score a goal.

Pat: Yes, he's a real hot dog.

A **hot potato,** on the other hand, means trouble.
Imagine taking a baked potato out of the oven with

your bare hands. You'd probably put it down quickly! A hot potato is something that you want to get rid of or avoid.

Mrs. Laws: Are you going to the school board meeting tonight?

Mr. Chips: No, I don't want to be there. Everyone is going to fight about the new graduation requirements.

Mrs. Laws: The new requirements are a real hot potato, but I think we should go. We have to tell the board our opinions.

There are many idioms about keeping and telling secrets. When you spill a pot of beans, everyone can see them. When you **spill the beans,** you tell a secret. You tell something that you weren't supposed to tell.

Geoffrey: How was Carolyn's surprise party?

Chris: It wasn't a surprise. Jen spilled the beans. She accidentally told Carolyn about it.

Now it's time to be an egghead and get the correct answers to the exercises. (An **egghead** is an intelligent, educated person.)

A. What do you say? Circle the correct sentence.

EXERCISES

David added extra facts to the story.

a. He has a hot potato.

(*b.*) He beefed it up.

1. Frank studies all the time.

   a. He's a hot potato.

   b. He's an egghead.

2. Carla told the secret.

   a. She spilled the beans.

   b. She hammed it up.

3. Steve ate the whole pie.

   a. He had other fish to fry.

   b. He made a pig of himself.

4. They added more rice to the soup.

   a. They hammed it up.

   b. They beefed it up.

5. That actor always exaggerates.

   a. He's an egghead.

   b. He's a ham.

6. Ruth always has a million things to do.

   a. She has other fish to fry.

   b. She spills the beans.

7. Everyone argues about this problem.

   a. It's a hot dog.

   b. It's a hot potato.

8. Carol acts silly when she recites in front of the class.

   a. She hams it up.

   b. She beefs it up.

9. The player jumped up and down after he caught the ball.

   a. He's a hot dog.

   b. He's an egghead.

10. We wanted Bob to come with us, but he can't.

    a. He makes a pig of himself.

    b. He has other fish to fry.

B. Complete the sentence with one of the idioms. You may use an idiom more than once.

a hot dog	beef up
a hot potato	make a pig of yourself
a ham	have other fish to fry
an egghead	ham it up
	spill the beans

Ellen and Tony don't have time to play cards. They **have other fish to fry** _____.

1. Please be serious, Bob. Don't always _____

    _____.

2. You're sick because you ate too much. I told you

    not to _____.

3. Lynn always overacts. She's _____

    _____.

4. Jay found out the answers to the test. Do you

    think he'll _____ to the rest

    of the class?

5. The gardens at the museum look terrible. The

    museum director should _____

    _____ the gardening staff.

6. Bill and Brian never spend time with their

    family. They always _____

    _____.

7. Laura always gets good grades. She's _____

   _____.

8. Timmy always rides his bike "no hands." He's

   _____.

9. Nobody agrees about this problem. It's _____

   _____.

10. Let's _____ this soup with

    some chopped vegetables.

DISCUSSION

1. Think of your favorite television shows. Name a character who is each of these: a hot dog, a ham, a top banana, an egghead, someone who always has other fish to fry.

2. Write a short paragraph. Tell about someone who spills the beans.

3. List several famous people who you think are hot dogs. Share your list with the class. Do your classmates agree with you?

4. List five things or situations that you think are hot potatoes. Exchange your list with a classmate. Choose a thing on the list you are holding and write a sentence about it. Do you think it's a hot potato, too?

5. Go to the literature section of the library. Find a book of poems in English. Look for a short poem with a food in the title. Read the poem in class. Discuss its meaning.

the apple of (one's) eye	as American as apple pie
apple polisher/apple polishing	in apple-pie order
an egghead	thin-skinned
a ham	
a hot dog	to beef up
a hot potato	to compare apples and oranges
a lemon	to get to the core of
a peach	to go bananas
a peaches-and-cream complexion	to go to pieces
sour grapes	to ham it up
the top banana	to have other fish to fry
a tough nut to crack	to hear it through the grapevine
	to make a pig of (oneself)
one bad apple spoils the barrel	to spill the beans

A. Circle the correct answer.

Who exaggerate to be funny?

(a.) people who ham it up

b. people who go to pieces

1. Who eat too much?

    a. people who make pigs of themselves

    b. people who go bananas

2. Who always have other things to do?

    a. people who get to the core of things

    b. people who have other fish to fry

3. Who tell secrets?

    a. people who spill the beans

    b. people who hear it through the grapevine

4. Who often have hurt feelings?

    a. people who are thin-skinned

    b. people who are tough nuts to crack

5. Who know which side their bread is buttered on?

    a. people who are apple polishers

    b. people who have peaches-and-cream complexions

6. Who is the boss?

    a. a lemon

    b. the top banana

7. Who is loveable?

    a. a hot dog

    b. a peach

8. Who overacts?

    a. a hot potato

    b. a ham

9. Who is a favorite?

    a. a ham

    b. the apple of someone's eye

10. Who is smart?

    a. an egghead

    b. a lemon

B. Match the idiom with its meaning.

__e__	1.	something that doesn't work
_____	2.	someone who shows off
_____	3.	something to avoid
_____	4.	neat
_____	5.	sensitive
_____	6.	made in the U.S.A.
_____	7.	someone who flatters
_____	8.	someone who is difficult
_____	9.	someone who is intelligent
_____	10.	someone who is a honey

a. an apple polisher

b. an egghead

c. a hot dog

d. a hot potato

e. a lemon

f. a peach

g. a tough nut to crack

h. as American as apple pie

i. in apple-pie order

j. thin-skinned

C. Complete the sentence. Use an idiom.

I told her I didn't like her new haircut. Now she's crying. She's really __**thin-skinned**_____.

1. June accidentally told Sam's secret. She didn't

   mean to _____.

2. He always acts silly when people are watching.

   He likes to _____.

3. When he hears the good news, he's going to _____

   _____.

4. When she hears the bad news, she's going to _____

   _____.

5. I'm sorry you have a stomachache, but I told you

   not to _____

   _____ yourself.

6. How can you say that playing tennis is more fun

   than reading a book? You're _____

   _____.

7. Alex failed the test, so he said that Mrs. Scott is

   a bad teacher. It's just _____.

8. My cousin has beautiful skin. She has a _____

   _____.

9. Timmy always makes trouble. He gets the other

   children to misbehave. His teacher says, "_____

   _____."

10. Jimmy never makes trouble. He's the teacher's

    favorite. His teacher says, "He's _____

    _____."

AS FLAT AS A PANCAKE

to make a hash of (something)

out to lunch

a bad egg/a good egg

to lay an egg

to egg someone on

to walk on eggs

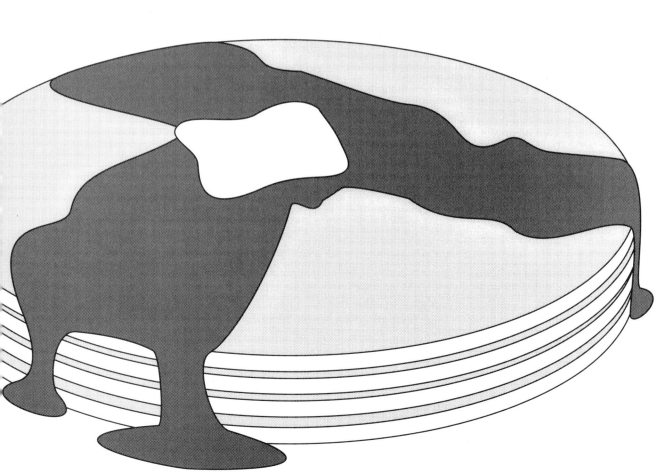

READING

A pancake is supposed to be flat, but most cakes are not. A flat cake is a baker's mistake or failure. Many of the idioms in this unit are about making mistakes or being wrong. Some of them describe people who are bad or wrong.

Hash is an old American food. You make it by mixing chopped-up meat and potatoes. You can use meat and potatoes left over from another meal. **To make a hash of something** means "to ruin it or change it so no one can use it."

Old MacDonald: Mary, where are my sheep? I can't find them.

Mary Contrary: They ran away. First they chewed up the vegetables and made a hash of my flower garden. Then they pulled all the laundry off the line. You'd better find them and put them back in their pen, or I'll make a hash of them!

Here is another way to use this idiom. It describes someone who doesn't do his or her work well.

Judge: Mr. Flaw! I don't ever want to see you in my courtroom again!

Lawyer: Why not? My client was acquitted.

Judge: Yes, but you made a hash of the defense. She almost went to jail. You didn't help her very much.

When people leave their offices, they sometimes put signs on the doors. The signs might say "on vacation" or "out of town until Monday." Another sign might say "out to lunch." All of these signs mean "nobody is here."

When we say that a person is **out to lunch,** we mean that he or she isn't very smart or that he or she does foolish things. We say that the person acts as if he or she is "not all there."

Harris: I can't believe that Barney did that!

Miller: What did he do? Why are you shouting?

Harris: He told a customer that this limousine is on sale. We can't sell it for that low price. He's totally out to lunch!

Miller: Sometimes Barney goes nuts when he sees a good-looking customer.

A spoiled or bad egg smells and tastes awful. A person who is **a bad egg** is a person who behaves badly. **A good egg,** on the other hand, is a good person.

Wendy: Mr. Hook looks so mean. He scares me.

Peter: He's not such a bad egg. He helped me fix my bike when it broke.

Wendy: Maybe he's a good egg after all.

To lay an egg means to fail.

Usher: Do you hear the audience? They're really
            laughing!

Customer: Yes. The play must be a great success.

Usher: Are you kidding? It's supposed to be
            serious! It's laying an egg.

When you **egg someone on,** you encourage them
to do something they don't want to do. To egg someone
on is rude and not kind.

Tai: Why did you try to jump over all those
          barrels?

Randy: I didn't want to, but Dick kept egging me on.

Tai: You shouldn't listen to him. You know that
          one bad apple spoils the barrel.

Al: Hey! Have you gone bananas? Why did you hit me?

Joe: You kept egging me on. My hair is my business, not yours!

Al: I should have guessed it. Anyone with long hair is looking for trouble.

Joe: There you go—egging me on again!

Do you understand the idioms, or will you have to walk on eggs when you do the exercises? (**To walk on eggs** means "to be very careful.")

Mr. Block is in a bad mood. We'd better walk on eggs today!

EXERCISES   **A. Circle the correct answer to each question.**

Who do people like?

(a.) a good egg

b. a bad egg

1. Who failed?

    a. the one who laid an egg

    b. the one who walked on eggs

2. Who isn't very smart?

    a. the one who is a good egg

    b. the one who is out to lunch

3. Who ruined something?

    a. the one who walked on eggs

    b. the one who made a hash of it

4. Who was very cautious?

    a. the one who walked on eggs

    b. the one who egged someone on

5. Who might be "the one bad apple who spoils the barrel"?

    a. the one who is a good egg

    b. the one who eggs someone on

6. Who spoiled the plan?

    a. the one who was out to lunch

    b. the one who made a hash of it

7. Who might act foolish?

    a. the one who walks on eggs

    b. the one who is out to lunch

8. Who would you hire to work for you?

    a. the one who is a good egg

    b. the one who makes a hash of things

9. Who might go bananas?

    a. the one who is a good egg

    b. the one who is egged on

10. Who got a goose egg?

    a. the one who walked on eggs

    b. the one who laid an egg

B. Complete the sentence with one of the idioms. Use the past tense. (See Alphabetical Index.)

is a bad egg	egg me on	make a hash of
is out to lunch	lay an egg	walk on eggs

I didn't believe him. I thought he **was a bad egg**_____.

1. He ruined all our plans. He _____

    _____ them.

2. Her idea was a complete failure. She really

    _____.

3. Our teacher last year was very thin-skinned. We

    _____ in her class.

4. Marty wasn't paying attention. When the teacher

    called on him, he _____.

5. I didn't want to break the window. Tommy told

   me to do it. He _____.

DISCUSSION

1. Choose a dialogue from this unit and rewrite it without the idiom. Keep the same meaning. Is your dialogue longer or shorter than the one in the book? How do idioms change the length of a sentence? Discuss.

2. Some of the idioms in this unit are not polite. When are they impolite? Reread Unit 1 for some ideas.

3. Make a list of the idioms in this unit. Think of a one-word definition for each idiom. Share your definitions with the class.

4. Rewrite this TV commercial without any idioms. Read it to the class. Which commercial sounds more interesting?

   "Do you want to stop making a hash of your life? Are you tired of hearing people say, 'You're out to lunch'? Do people often tell you, 'You laid an egg'? Then call 1-800-555-5000 and order our Handy-Dandy-Organizer-Notebook! This calendar/checklist/shopping list/address book costs only $19.95. Use it and you will become the top banana in your company! Your friends will call you the salt of the earth! You'll remember appointments, birthdays, chores. You'll never be small potatoes again!"

UNIT EIGHT
PIE IN
THE SKY

pie in the sky

the upper crust

to have crust/crusty

to eat humble pie

as easy as pie

to have a finger in
every pie

gravy/on the gravy train

READING

This unit includes idioms about pie and gravy. But you can't eat the pie, and you won't find the gravy on the dinner table!

Pie in the sky describes something that you think will not happen or something that you will probably not get.

Mother: What do you want to be when you grow up?

Ronnie: I want to be a movie star. Then I want to be President of the United States.

Mother: Oh, Ronnie, be realistic. That's just pie in the sky.

Some pies have two crusts—one on the bottom and one on the top. Sometimes we call important or rich people **the upper crust.** This is an informal, joking way of saying "upper class" or "high society." Many Americans believe that money is the one thing that determines class.

Morgan: Do you really want to buy a condominium in this expensive building?

Myrna: Of course. Now that we have so much money, I want to join the upper crust!

Morgan: Do you think money is enough to make us
         upper class?

Mryna: It's a start. We'll get season tickets to the
         opera, and join a charitable organization,
         and send the children to the best schools,
         and . . .

Morgan: Stop! I'm tired already! Being upper crust is
         hard work!

Crust is also the word for the hard, outside part of
bread. A person who **has crust** is bold or impudent.
He or she might be aggressive or rude.

Casper: Did you see that? Milton pushed his way to
         the front of the line!

George: He has a lot of crust! He should wait his
         turn like everybody else!

People who are **crusty** might act rough and tough,
but they are not necessarily bad. They might speak in
a gruff or unfriendly way, or they might use colorful
or "salty" language. (*Salty* can mean "brief and witty."
It can also mean "vulgar" or "improper.") We usually
use this idiom to describe older people.

Ahab: I'll bet that crusty old sailor tells a lot of good
        stories.

Dick: Yes, he does. And he uses very salty language!

When you **eat humble pie,** you admit that you are
wrong. To eat humble pie is disagreeable and
humiliating. For example, imagine that you did
something bad, and you tried to hide it. Now other
people know about it. You have to confess. You're very
embarrassed, but you eat humble pie and admit that
you were wrong.

Sunny: Why did Manny lie about me?

Laura: He's jealous of you. He didn't get promoted,
        and you did.

Sunny: He has to tell the truth now, or I'll get fired!

Laura: Don't worry. I'll talk to him. I'll tell him to go
        to the boss and eat humble pie.

As easy as pie means the same as *a piece of cake*
and *duck soup.* It means "very, very easy."

Harpo: That test was as easy as pie!

Zeppo: A piece of cake!

Groucho: Duck soup!

People who are always busy **have a finger in
every pie.** In this idiom, *pie* means "activity" or
"thing that is happening."

Sally: Dick, can you help with the Boy Scout lunch
        on Saturday?

Dick: Sure, but I'll be a little late. I have to coach
        the girls' softball team at 7 A.M. And I'm going
        to a committee meeting at 10.

Sally: You certainly have a finger in every pie!

Gravy is a sauce for meat and potatoes. You make it from the juice that comes out of meat in cooking. Gravy is something extra. **Gravy** is a slang word for profit. When you are **on the gravy train,** you receive money for little or no work.

Jean: How is your cookie sale doing?

Lynn: Great! We made enough money this morning to pay for all the ingredients. From now on, it's all gravy.

Mark: Where did Harry get that new car?

Bob: His rich uncle died and left him a lot of money. He's on the gravy train now!

Are you ready for the exercises? Will you find them as easy as pie? Or will you have to eat humble pie and admit that you didn't study?

EXERCISES

A. Choose the correct idiom to complete the sentence.

1. She always has other fish to fry. She has ___e___.

2. He cooked his own goose when he lied. Now he has to _____.

3. She's so rich that she doesn't have to work for her bread and butter. She's _____.

4. That test was a piece of cake. It was _____.

5. Did that stranger call you "honey"? He really _____.

   a. on the gravy train

   b. as easy as pie

   c. has crust

   d. eat humble pie

   e. a finger in every pie

B. Complete the sentence with one of the idioms.

pie in the sky   on the gravy train
the upper crust   eat humble pie
gravy   has crust
as easy as pie   has a finger in every pie
crusty

When I win the lottery, I want to sail around the world. Unfortunately, it's probably **pie in the sky** _____.

1. He had to say he was sorry.

   He had to _____.

2. They're rich now.

   They're _____ now.

3. That old farmer acts tough, but he's really a good egg. That old farmer is a _____

   _____ person.

4. Doing this exercise is duck soup.

   Doing this exercise is _____.

5. She belongs to a lot of groups and does many

   things. She _____.

6. He's very rude and aggressive!

   He _____.

7. The Smyth-Worthingtons are jet-setters.

   They're members of _____.

8. I want to be a famous rock star and find a cure

   for cancer, but it probably won't happen.

   I want to be a famous rock star and find a cure

   for cancer, but it's probably _____

   _____.

9. I forgot to do my homework! When the teacher

   asks for it, I'll have to admit it.

   I forgot to do my homework! When the teacher

   asks for it, I'll have to _____

   _____.

10. I earned enough yesterday to pay my expenses.

    The money I earn today will all be profit.

    The money I earn today will be _____

    _____.

DISCUSSION

1. When a young person says something harsh, we might say he or she has crust. When an older person says something harsh, we might say he or she is crusty. Why do you think this is so? What's the difference between "having crust" and being "crusty"?

2. Do you know someone who has a finger in every pie? What other idioms can you use to describe that person?

3. What do you think it takes to be a member of the upper crust? Explain.

4. Pretend that you're on the gravy train. What will you do? (Will you work? Go to school? Travel?) What will you buy? (A big house? A fancy car? Jewelry?)

5. You and a classmate make up a dialogue that shows the meaning of "pie in the sky." Perform the dialogue for the class.

ON A ROLL

on a roll

bread/dough

to bring home the bacon

a baker's dozen

to reach (one's) boiling point

to simmer down

to burn out

the greatest thing since sliced bread

READING

This unit dishes up bread and bacon, but you can't eat them. Then it describes activities that sound like cooking hints. But these idioms are about feelings, not cooking.

The word *roll* has many meanings. When you roll something, you move it. You turn it over and over. A roll is something you eat. It is bread that is rolled and baked.

To be **on a roll** means that good things are happening to you quickly and often. Everything is panning out. When something rolls, it moves fast. When you are on a roll, you are quickly moving toward success.

Pat: This author is really successful! This is her third best-selling book this year!

Ken: Yes, she's really on a roll!

Everybody is interested in money. Maybe that's why there are so many slang words for money. You bake dough to make bread. **Dough** and **bread** are both slang words for money. People feel that money is as basic and necessary to life as bread is. Words like these are informal and should not be used in business conversations. *Lettuce* and *cabbage* are other old American slang words for money. Why? Because American money is green.

When you earn your bread and butter, you bring home the bacon. **To bring home the bacon** means "to bring home or earn money." In this idiom, bacon stands for all food, clothing, and other things that are necessary.

Freddie: Do you want to go to the bank with me? I'm going to deposit my paycheck.

Flossie: No. I'm on my way to buy a lottery ticket. That's how I plan to bring home the bacon!

Freddie: Do you ever win?

Flossie: Well, no. But I might!

Freddie: That's just pie in the sky! If you get a job, you can bring home the bacon every week.

There are twelve items in a dozen. Sometimes when you buy a dozen rolls or cookies, the baker gives you thirteen. He or she does this to attract more customers. **A baker's dozen** means thirteen of anything.

Fred: I'd like to buy some roses.

Ginger: Certainly, sir. We have a special today. You can get a baker's dozen for the price of twelve.

Fred: Fine. I'll take twelve. I mean thirteen.

When you heat a liquid, it boils. Bubbles explode on the surface. When a person **reaches the boiling point,** he or she is ready to explode with anger.

When something is boiling and you turn down the heat, it cooks more slowly. No bubbles explode on the surface. It's simmering. When someone is boiling with anger, you might say, **"Simmer down."** This means "calm yourself."

Mother: That's it! I've reached the boiling point! Carl is late for dinner again!

Father: Simmer down, honey. He's probably busy at school. You know he has a finger in every pie.

Mother: I know, but he should call when he's going to be late.

Burned things are usually no good. You can't eat burned food. It won't give you energy. When wood is burning, it keeps people warm. But after it burns, it doesn't give heat. It has no energy left. When people **burn out,** they have no energy or enthusiasm left. They are tired of doing something, and they don't want to do that job or activity any more.

Teacher: I'm not coming back to teach next year. I'm going to get a different job.

Principal: Are you sure? You're a great teacher! We need you.

Teacher: I can't. I'm burned out. I need a rest.

Principal: I'm sorry to see you go. Let me know if you change your mind.

Are you burned out on cooking idioms? Then you might find the exercises **the greatest thing since sliced bread.** (In the United States, most people buy sliced bread in packages. This idiom describes anything that is new and good. The idiom is so common that people make up variations; for example, "the greatest thing since bottled beer.")

EXERCISES

A. Circle the correct answer to each question.

Who gets promoted quickly?

(a.) the one who is on a roll

b. the one who simmers down

1. Who is tired of his or her job?

    a. the one who is burned out

    b. the one who is on a roll

2. Who is angry?

    a. the one who brings home the bacon

    b. the one who reaches the boiling point

3. Who is very successful?

    a. the one who simmers down

    b. the one who is on a roll

4. Who earns money?

    a. the one who brings home the bacon

    b. the one who burns out

5. Who stops being angry?

    a. the one who is on a roll

    b. the one who simmers down

B. Complete each sentence with one of the idioms. Use the past tense in numbers 1–4.

bring home the bacon	a baker's dozen
burn out	on a roll
reach the boiling point	the greatest thing since
simmer down	sliced bread

You gave me thirteen donuts.
You gave me **a baker's dozen**   .

1. Mr. Jones got very angry. He _____

    _____.

2. Finally, Mr. Jones became calm. He _____

    _____.

3. Mr. Jones earned a paycheck every week. He _____

    _____.

4. After twenty years, Mr. Jones got tired of his job.

   He _____.

5. Mr. Jones had three job offers this week. He's ____

   _____.

6. Mr. Jones loves his new job. He thinks it's _____

   _____.

DISCUSSION

1. If you started a wall chart of idioms, look at it now. Can you divide the idioms into idea groups? Some examples might be *money, trust,* and *anger.* Label each group of idioms.

2. Select a dialogue from this unit. Ask a friend to read it with you. Practice your expression and pronunciation. Read it to the class. Ask the other students if you expressed the feeling in the dialogue correctly.

3. Do you know any slang words for money in another language? Share them with the class. Why do you think those words are used for money?

4. Why do you think people burn out? What kinds of jobs might make people burn out? Discuss your ideas with the class.

5. What makes you reach your boiling point? What makes you simmer down? Compare your feelings with your classmates'.

6. What do you think is the greatest thing since sliced bread? Make up an "idiom." Some examples might be "the greatest thing since color television" or "the greatest thing since blue jeans."

SWEETS FOR THE SWEET

to have (one's) cake and eat it, too

to take the cake

the frosting on the cake

a smart cookie / a tough cookie

like taking candy from a baby

everything from soup to nuts

READING

Candy, cake, and cookies are sweets. A meal often ends with something sweet. This book ends with sweet-sounding idioms.

To have your cake and eat it, too means "to want too much." We use this idiom to say, "You can't have everything." (If you eat your cake, you don't have it any longer.)

Adele: What's the matter?

Tom: I need a new car. But if I buy one, I won't have enough money to go on vacation.

Adele: Well, you'll have to decide. You can't have your cake and eat it, too.

Someone or something that **takes the cake** upsets people. A hundred years ago, a cakewalk was a kind of dance contest. The winner of a cakewalk often got a cake as a prize. *To take the cake* meant "to win first place." Now we use this idiom to mean "I don't believe it!"

Rosie: Did you see this story about us in the newspaper? That reporter changed everything I said!

Gabriel: He really takes the cake! We invited him into our home. We gave him dinner. And he lied about us!

Rosie: I'm going to sue him! He's a bad egg!

Frosting is the sweet topping on a cake. **The frosting on the cake** is an extra part that makes something good even better. For example, you were happy when the boss gave you a raise. When she named you "employee of the year," it was the frosting on the cake.

Reporter: How do you feel about winning the Academy Award?

Actress: Just being nominated was an honor.
           Getting the Oscar was the frosting on the
           cake!

A cookie is a small, flat, sweet cake. *Cookie* is a
slang word for a person. It is usually slightly critical.
A smart cookie is intelligent but may be a hot dog. A
smart cookies usually knows which side his or her
bread is buttered on. **A tough cookie** might have
crust. He or she is probably a tough nut to crack.

It is easy to take something from a baby. A baby
can't fight to keep the thing. When we say something
is **like taking candy from a baby,** we mean it's very
easy. It's as easy as pie.

Betty: Did your grandmother lend you her car?

Veronica: Yes. We can use it all day.

Betty: *My* grandmother won't lend me *her* car.
           How did you do it?

Veronica: My grandmother likes me a lot. It was like
           taking candy from a baby.

In this example, it means "taking something that
doesn't belong to you."

Robber #1: Did you get their money?

Robber #2: Sure. I got jewelry, too.

Robber #1: Did they give you any trouble?

Robber #2: No. They were scared. It was like taking candy from a baby.

Soup is often the first part of a big meal. Nuts can be the dessert or the last part of a meal. The idiom **everything from soup to nuts** means "from beginning to end" or "a wide variety of things." An office worker might file, type, answer the phone, write reports, make out the budget, etc. He or she does everything from soup to nuts. You might be able to buy a wide variety of things in a certain store—tools, dishes, clothes, books, etc. That store sells everything from soup to nuts.

This book contains idioms about everything from soup to nuts. You now know a lot about English. Doing the exercises will be the frosting on the cake!

EXERCISES

A. Draw a circle around the correct answer.

Who might be described as a smart cookie?

a. an egghead

b. a baker's dozen

1. Who might be as cool as a cucumber?

    a. a tough cookie

    b. the frosting on the cake

2. What's like taking candy from a baby?

    a. chicken feed

    b. a piece of cake

3. Who knows which side his bread is buttered on?

    a. duck soup

    b. a smart cookie

4. Who might be a bad egg?

    a. someone who takes the cake

    b. the frosting on the cake

5. Who might have crust?

    a. a baker's dozen

    b. a tough cookie

B. What do you say? Write the correct sentence.

That takes the cake!
You can't have your cake and eat it, too.
It was like taking candy from a baby.
They did everything from soup to nuts.
It was the frosting on the cake!

They had many different kinds of jobs.
They did everything from soup to nuts.
_____

1. Something was very, very easy.

    _____

2. Something was extra special.

    _____

3. Your friends did all the work in the office today.

    _____

4. Someone did something that surprised you.

    _____

5. Someone wants more than he or she can have.

    _____

DISCUSSION

1. How many idioms can you remember that mean "very easy"? List them and use each one in a sentence. Read your sentences to the class.

2. Idioms and slang are informal English. Discuss times when you should probably *not* use idioms.

3. Divide the class into teams of four. Each team should select an idea group of idioms. Each team should then write a short, four person dialogue. Use as many of the idioms as possible in the dialogue. Read or perform your dialogue for the class.

4. Name something that you thought was the frosting on the cake. Why did you feel that way?

5. Choose your favorite idiom in this book. Write a short paragraph about it. Why do you like that idiom the best? Read your paragraph to the class.

a bad egg

a baker's dozen

bread

dough

everything from soup to nuts

the frosting on the cake

a good egg

gravy

the greatest thing since sliced bread

a smart cookie

a tough cookie

the upper crust

as easy as pie

crusty

like taking candy from a baby

on the gravy train

out to lunch

to be on a roll

to bring home the bacon

to burn out

to eat humble pie

to egg someone on

to have a finger in every pie

to have crust

to have your cake and eat it, too

to lay an egg

to make a hash of something

to reach one's boiling point

to simmer down

to take the cake

to walk on eggs

A. Circle the correct answer.

Who is not as angry as before?

a. the one who is simmering down

b. the one who is burning out

1. Who is not successful?
   a. the one who is on the gravy train
   b. the one who lays an egg

2. Who makes people angry?
   a. the one who brings home the bacon
   b. the one who eggs them on

3. Who is successful?

    a. the one who is on a roll

    b. the one who is out to lunch

4. Who earns money?

    a. the one who brings home the bacon

    b. the one who has a finger in every pie

5. Who wants too much?

    a. the one who makes a hash of something

    b. the one who wants to have his cake and eat it, too

6. Who takes the cake?

    a. the one who has crust

    b. the one who simmers down

7. Who might use salty language?

    a. the one who walks on eggs

    b. the one who is crusty

8. Who admits he was wrong?

    a. the one who burns out

    b. the one who eats humble pie

9. Who is very busy?

    a. the one who has a finger in every pie

    b. the one who is out to lunch

10. Who becomes angry?

    a. the one who reaches the boiling point

    b. the one who takes the cake

11. Who might you *not* trust?

    a. a bad egg

    b. the upper crust

12. Who do you want for a friend?

    a. a smart cookie

    b. a good egg

13. Who knows which side her bread is buttered on?

    a. a baker's dozen

    b. a smart cookie

14. What is something extra?

    a. everything from soup to nuts

    b. the frosting on the cake

15. What is new and wonderful?

    a. the upper crust

    b. the greatest thing since sliced bread

B. Match the idiom with its meaning.

__j__	1. baker's dozen	*a.*	as easy as pie
_____	2. bread	*b.*	exhausted
_____	3. burned out	*c.*	fail
_____	4. crusty	*d.*	foolish
_____	5. gravy	*e.*	high society
_____	6. lay an egg	*f.*	money
_____	7. like taking candy from a baby	*g.*	profit
_____	8. on a roll	*h.*	salty
_____	9. out to lunch	*i.*	successful
_____	10. the upper crust	*j.*	thirteen

C. Complete the sentence. Use one of the idioms.

She has to stop being angry.
She has to **simmer down**   .

1. He has to be very careful.

   He has to _____.

2. She has to become calm.

   She has to _____.

3. He has to get a job.

   He has to _____.

4. She has to admit that she was wrong.

   She has to _____.

5. He wants to have everything.

   He wants to _____.

6. She's getting very angry.

   She's going to _____.

7. He's going to ruin everything.

   He's going to _____ it.

8. She's going to fail.

   She's going to _____.

9. He's going to become exhausted.

   He's going to _____.

10. She's going to start a fight with him.

    She's going to _____.

Circle the correct answer or answers

Something easy

(a.) duck soup

(b.) a piece of cake

c. nuts

What is it?

1. Money
   a. dough
   b. sour grapes
   c. bread

2. A little money
   a. gravy
   b. chicken feed
   c. crust

3. A profit
   a. the upper crust
   b. a hot potato
   c. gravy

4. Nothing
   a. a goose egg
   b. the frosting on the cake
   c. nuts

5. Thirteen
   a. duck soup
   b. the salt of the earth
   c. a baker's dozen

6. High society
   a. sugar
   b. apple polishing
   c. the upper crust

7. Pretty skin
   a. honey
   b. a peaches-and-cream complexion
   c. everything from soup to nuts

8. A problem
   a. a hot dog
   b. a ham
   c. a hot potato

9. A thank-you note
   a. a bread-and-butter letter
   b. the gravy train
   c. a tough cookie

10. Something extra

    a. one's bread and butter

    b. the frosting on the cake

    c. a good egg

11. Something that's not important

    a. sour grapes

    b. small potatoes

    c. nuts

12. Something that's not worth a hill of beans

    a. a peach

    b. a honey

    c. a lemon

13. Something that probably won't happen

    a. a piece of cake

    b. pie in the sky

    c. the apple of my eye

Who is it?

14. Who might make a hash of things?

    a. a chowderhead

    b. a smart cookie

    c. a butterfingers

15. Who might chicken out?

    a. chickenfeed

    b. a chicken

    c. small potatoes

16. Who knows which side his bread is buttered on?

    a. a smart cookie

    b. a goose egg

    c. an apple polisher

17. Who hams it up?

    a. a hot dog

    b. a hot potato

    c. the top banana

18. Who is the apple of someone's eye?

    a. a lemon

    b. a peach

    c. honey

19. Who is the salt of the earth?

    a. a piece of cake

    b. a butterfingers

    c. a good egg

20. Who is important?

    a. the top banana

    b. small potatoes

    c. sour grapes

21. Who is a bad actor?

    a. a chowderhead

    b. a ham

    c. a baker's dozen

22. Who is difficult?

    a. a tough nut to crack

    b. the upper crust

    c. a tough cookie

23. Who is calm?

    a. the one who is as cool as a cucumber

    b. the one who simmered down

    c. the one who apple polishes

24. Who is upset?

    a. the one who talks turkey

    b. the one who goes to pieces

    c. the one who reaches the boiling point

25. Who acts crazy?

    a. the one who is as nutty as a fruitcake

    b. the one who is the top banana

    c. the one who goes bananas

26. Who is successful?

    a. the one who is on a roll

    b. the one who is on the gravy train

    c. the one who is small potatoes

27. Who fails?

    a. the one who adds some spice to her life

    b. the one who lays an egg

    c. the one who makes a hash of it

28. Who has a steady job?

    a. the one who earns his bread and butter

    b. the one who brings home the bacon

    c. the one who takes the cake

29. Who acts foolish?

    a. the one who is out to lunch

    b. the one who eats like a bird

    c. the one who eats humble pie

30. Who is busy?

    a. the one who has other fish to fry

    b. the one who has crust

    c. the one who has a finger in every pie

31. Who is sensitive?

    a. the one who is crusty

    b. the one who is a tough cookie

    c. the one who is thin-skinned

What did he or she do?

32. She stopped without help.

    a. She talked turkey.

    b. She quit cold turkey.

    c. She laid an egg.

33. He told a secret.

    a. He burned out.

    b. He had crust.

    c. He spilled the beans.

34. She told him all the answers.

    a. She spoon-fed him.

    b. She egged him on.

    c. She hammed it up.

35. He learned some gossip.

    a. He heard it through the grapevine.

    b. He had other fish to fry.

    c. He simmered down.

36. She was very careful.

    a. She took the cake.

    b. She walked on eggs.

    c. She ate humble pie.

37. He added rice to the soup.

    a. He took the cake.

    b. He dished it out.

    c. He beefed it up.

38. She solved the problem.

    a. She compared apples and oranges.

    b. She got to the core of it.

    c. She added some spice to her life.

39. He got into worse trouble.

    a. He wrote a bread-and-butter letter.

    b. He went out of the frying pan into the fire.

    c. He dished it up.

40. She was serious.

    a. She talked turkey.

    b. She chickened out.

    c. She went bananas.

What do you say?

41. You don't like something.

    a. "It's not my cup of tea."

    b. "It's the greatest thing since sliced bread."

    c. "It's duck soup."

42. Something is easy.

    a. "It's a piece of cake."

    b. "It's as easy as pie."

    c. "It's a goose egg."

43. Someone is over-confident.

    a. "He's on the gravy train."

    b. "Don't count your chickens before they hatch."

    c. "He cooked his own goose."

44. Someone egged someone else on.

    a. "One bad apple spoils the barrel."

    b. "You can't have your cake and eat it, too."

    c. "It's the frosting on the cake."

45. Something is not difficult.

    a. "It's not worth a hill of beans."

    b. "It's duck soup."

    c. "It's like taking candy from a baby."

46. A thief has the jewelry. You're a police officer.

    a. "Fork it over!"

    b. "Let's talk turkey."

    c. "Simmer down."

47. Someone ate too much.

    a. "She ate like a bird."

    b. "She ate humble pie."

    c. "She made a pig of herself."

48. Something failed.

    a. "It didn't pan out."

    b. "It laid an egg."

    c. "It was all gravy."

49. Something is neat and clean.

    a. "It's not worth a hill of beans."

    b. "It's my bread and butter."

    c. "It's in apple-pie order."

50. Someone says something. You don't believe it.

    a. "He's on a roll."

    b. "Take it with a grain of salt."

    c. "It's as American as apple pie."

NOTIONAL INDEX

**Numbers indicate Units
"I" indicates Introduction**

Revelation
hear it through the grapevine   5
to spill the beans   6

Sensitivity (compare *insensitivity*)
thin-skinned   5

Seriousness
to talk turkey   3

Success (compare *failure*)
to pan out   1
on a roll   9

Sycophancy
apple polisher   4
apple polishing   4
to know which side (one's) bread is
    buttered on   2

Trouble
to cook (one's) own goose   3
to go out of the frying pan into the
    fire   1

Trustworthiness
a good egg   7
a peach   5
the salt of the earth   2

Unimportance (compare *importance*)
small potatoes   I

Worthlessness (compare *money*)
a bad egg   7
chicken feed   I
a goose egg   3
a lemon   5
not worth a hill of beans   I

ALPHABETICAL INDEX WITH PARTS OF VERBS

Numbers indicate Units
"I" indicates Introduction

Expression	Parts of verbs (present, past, past participle)	Unit
to add some spice to (one's) life	add, added, added	2
the apple of (one's) eye		4
apple polisher		4
apple polishing		4
as American as apple pie		4
as cool as a cucumber		I
as easy as pie		8
as nutty as a fruitcake		I
a bad egg		7
a baker's dozen		9
to beef up	beef, beefed, beefed	6
to bring home the bacon	bring, brought, brought	9
to burn out	burn, burned, burned	9
a butterfingers		2
bread		9
(one's) bread and butter		2
a bread-and-butter letter		2
a chicken		3

nuts		I
on a roll		9
on the gravy train		8
one bad apple spoils the barrel	spoil, spoiled, spoiled	4
out to lunch		7
to pan out	pan, panned, panned	1
a peach		5
a peaches-and-cream complexion		5
pie in the sky		8
a piece of cake		3
to quit cold turkey	quit, quit, quit	3
to reach (one's) boiling point	reach, reached, reached	9
the salt of the earth		2
a smart cookie		10
to simmer down	simmer, simmered, simmered	9
small potatoes		I
sour grapes		5
to spill the beans	spill, spilled, spilled	6
to spoon-feed	spoon-feed, spoon-fed, spoon-fed	1
sugar		2
to take the cake	take, took, taken	10
to take it with a grain of salt	take, took, taken	2
to talk turkey	talk, talked, talked	3
thin-skinned		5
the top banana		5
a tough cookie		10
a tough nut to crack		5
the upper crust		8
to walk on eggs	walk, walked, walked	7